Tropiline Bajan Design

Tropiline from concept to development to pre-production

DON J.B. BLACKMAN

ISBN: 0615759211

ISBN 13:   9780615759210

Library of Congress Control Number: 2013902053
CreateSpace Independent Publishing Platform
North Charleston, South Carolina

Contents

Ferrari

Introduction

This is the chronicle of the design, development, and preproduction of the Tropiline Bajan Design (USA Design Patent Des 328198 S), which is arguably the best modern product design ever to come out of a small developing country (formerly Third World) and is a major advance in international modern art in the Western tradition with cultural, personal, and regional influences all synthesized to produce what is a humble work but a *masterpiece* all the same. It is a single line drawn in space as the essence of the design, like Kazimir Malevich's rotated linear squares, Eero Saarinen's Gateway Arch, and Constantine Brancusi's *Bird in Space*!

The design was twenty years ahead of its time. Although prototypes were made in Barbados and Denmark in the 1990s, the design remained mainly dormant until 2011 when it became active again due to the interest of a Chinese manufacturer who expressed an interest in producing and who then produced a number of prototypes in 2011 and 2012. The expected future commercial success of the design is testament to the design philosophy espoused here: that the major advances in Western art will come from incorporating creativity from the new economies, small states, and newcomers to the global art and design/industrial design stage.

This is modernism without reference to antiques, period pieces, and the like as the philosophical position that influenced every decision on form, materials, colors, finishes, textures, and presentation. The works of the modern masters, especially Eero Saarinen, Le Corbusier, and Marcel Breuer, were highly influential in pointing the direction forward both stylistically and, more importantly, philosophically. Mies Van der Rohe's mantra was "Less is more." Today, with the Tropiline design, I say, *"Even less is even more!"*

World Trade Center, New York

Times Square, New York

RCA (GE) Building, New York

Art School – New York: Design Philosophy 1980s

I studied architecture from 1982 to 1986 at a private art school in New York City. The prevailing design philosophy was modernism in the tradition of Bauhaus, Mies Van der Rohe, Walter Gropius, and Frank Lloyd Wright. However, even though there was no official doctrine or dogma that was mandated, a skillful student could select professors for the numerous required five-credit design courses over the five years to make sure that modern designers were the major influences. The greatest influences were Stanley Salzman, a Harvard-trained modernist; Gamal El-Zoghby, a geometric abstraction fanatic who made sure we did not leave his class with anything that would grace any *Home and Garden* magazine covers; and later Livio Dimitriu, who helped with the "sculptural abstraction with grace and poise process" (i.e. refinement), for my work was bold but a little too brutal! By the time I left art school, I was a geometric abstraction modernist, and my favorite living architects, for example, were American Richard Meier and Chinese I.M. Pei (both New York Whites). The New York Whites were a group of five architects who produced mainly slicked-up Le Corbusier buildings with very creative yet different personal styles. Their buildings were mostly white, hence the group's name.

But the art school was only a microcosm of New York City, which must be one of the best cities in the world in which to study architecture. Just one train ride, a few bus rides, and some walking from Brooklyn give firsthand experience of buildings of the magnificence of the then-World Trade Center (world's tallest building for many years), Empire State Building (formerly tallest building for decades), Frank Lloyd Wright's Guggenheim Museum (creative circular spiral organic ramp), Mies Van Der Rohe's Seagram Building (considered to be the perfect skyscraper in the rational modernist tradition), Chrysler Building (art deco masterpiece), Woolworth Building (Beaux-Arts showcase), and oddities like the Flatiron Building (with its acute triangular plan) from Broadway's collision with the Manhattan square grid street plan. Then there were the cathedrals; classical buildings like the Metropolitan Museum of Art, the contents of the Museum of Modern Art, and the Whitney Museum; and even postmodern masterpieces like the AT&T Building by Philip Johnson with its grandfather clock top!

Finally, New York architectural influences could not be discussed without reference to the numerous bridges around Manhattan, the most famous being the Brooklyn Bridge, which is pleasant to cross but did not impress me much (as a modernist) with its Gothic arches in the stone pylons. Why would a bridge that is a quarter-mile long with suspended steel cables as the structural method need to have Gothic brick arches that were used in the churches of Western Europe from hundreds of years before as its aesthetic expression?

You will see the influence of the purest bridge in New York City—the Verrazano-Narrows Bridge—on my work, with its clean, elegant towers, no brick patterning, mainly vertical cables supporting the roadway, and sweeping elevation. It presented a "breath of fresh air" compared to all other New York bridges with its elegant simplicity and visual structural brilliance.

Brooklyn Bridge (top) & Verrazano-Narrows Bridge, New York

Original Anaconda Chair, 1988

The original Tropiline chair was called the Anaconda chair after the snake, in that it wrapped itself around the user and traversed the body from one side to another in rotational symmetry in plan. What I did was to imagine in Caribbean culture that I was at the beach relaxing without a care in the world, hence the apparent "weightlessness" and sense of floating in space inherent in the design. As such the frame would not need to be traditional legs that carry load to the ground in a vertical perpendicular fashion. *The angled columns and sweeping fabric's curve came from the influence of Dulles airport. The rotational plan came from the influence of Le Corbusier's Carpenter Center at Harvard, Kenzo Tange's Olympic stadium in Tokyo, and Isamu Naguchi's coffee table, which has a complex series of transformations in its rotational symmetry.*

Over 99 percent of all furniture is usually symmetrical using simple reflective symmetry where what is on the right appears to be on the left (like a human face, a classical building, or the front grill of most luxury cars). Rotational symmetry gives balance but in a different way, looks more dynamic, is provocative and imaginative, but requires some skill to handle the resultant form's properties. For the layman it looks balanced, but they don't know why. For the design professional, it is balanced because of the use of one of the lesser used (but more advanced) forms of symmetry.

Rolls Royce

The Barbados Anaconda chair was patented in 1988 with Registered Industrial Design as number two. It was the second issued but the *first filed* and required a legal description of the design seen below. I went to considerable trouble to describe the line in great detail in terms of its shape, form, utility, and what was original, thus enough to justify being called an original work of art and design, a legal requirement for registration.

Barbados Patent

17 March 1988 original Barbados Patent application

Classes of Product: Furniture

Description: This product is a lounge chair frame that has <u>one continuous line</u> of tubing bent in a three-dimensional shape and a tensile material that fits over this frame.

The feature of the product that makes it original is the fact that the plan of the structure (the view from above looking vertically down) is the shape of the letter "S" or a reversed letter "S" with heightened and narrowed proportions, which are made of <u>one continuous line of tubing</u> with the two rounded ends elevated to form points for a tensile material to hook over. When the user rests in the chair in a horizontal position elevated from the ground level, the tubular frame starts from the ground under one's head then forms an arch inclined to the vertical plane with the top further away from the midpoint of the chair than the bottom. It then continues along one side of the body before turning and crossing over under the midsection of the body. The shape then turns toward the feet a short distance horizontally before forming an arch similar to that at the head which is inclined at an angle with the top further away from the midpoint of the chair than the bottom. The shape then terminates at the bottom of the arch after reaching ground level.

This shape is a three-dimensional object which can then support a hammock-type net, canvas, or other tensile material. The line can also consist of one piece of tubing sliding into another of a larger diameter to form a foldable chair. The intersection area is the straight area that is directly under the midsection of the body where the line crosses from one side of the body to another, i.e. left to right or vice versa (this location has been described in the paragraph above). This version has two holes drilled through the tubing at points on the intersection with shear-connecting bolts through them and nuts on the top. These nuts and bolts are connected to chains or looped wire and attached to the outside of the largest diameter tube for safety.

The chair can also be made any size larger than the standard seven-foot-long chair. Smaller sizes can also be constructed down to three feet in length for babies.

The possible materials for the chair frame are any <u>or</u> all of the following:

a. *Tubular metal*
b. *Plastic*

c. PVC

d. uPVC (unplastercised polyvinyl chloride)

e. Graphite

f. Laminated wood

g. Bentwood

h. Rattan

i. Glass

j. Lead crystal

k. Acrylic

Possible materials for the seating part are any or all of the following:

1. Canvas

2. Cloth

3. Leather

4. Wire net

5. Cord net

6. Beads tied with string

7. Fiberglass

8. Wood slats tied with string

9. Upholstered cushions

10. Bamboo tied with string

11. Cane rush

12. Rattan tied with laces

Executed March 15, 1988, and submitted March 17, 1988.

Influences – Modernist Architects

All modern architectural masters influenced the work. From Mies Van Der Rohe I learned restraint, balance, minimalism, and artistic editing in that it was not just pulling lines but the 3-D *perspective effect* of the lines drawn in plan that made for great spaces and products. Form follows function functionalism was the theoretical position. Also the intent was fit for purpose design in terms of lasting style versus current fashion. I tried for basic principles of formal manipulation of spaces where *"geometry is king"* and proportion his ever-attendant *"queen."*

Maserati

I. Eero Saarinen

Cruise Ship (top) and Dulles Airport, Washington, D.C.

Eero Saarinen used sculptural forms with a unique solution to a unique problem. Great examples are the Yale hockey rink with its dramatic roof, which I visited, and the MIT Kresge Auditorium dome, a one-eighth sphere brilliant structure and spatial solution. The structure defines the space versus some sort of applied decoration or ornament, as was done for classical, baroque, and rococo design from previous centuries.

Then there is the sweeping inverted arch of concrete draped like cloth for the roof of Dulles airport in Washington DC, with angled columns for the supports and with the angled "fist" connection of the columns to the roof. This influenced my chair design in its final form with the main elevation having a sweeping curve of canvas and angled columns for supports. *The purity and structural brilliance of Dulles airport was the greatest influence on the Tropiline, with Saarinen's Gateway Arch influencing the end elevation of the chair with the arch design.*

Antonio Roman on Saarinen: Eclecticism and the ability to combine pragmatic and existential concerns resonate strongly. Development of a consistent style was never a priority. Each design was a statement unto itself. A particular specific solution resolved by particular specific means. Dulles had concrete and suspension cable structure. He also fused the technical and the artistic. Saarinen's multiplicity was the ability to respond to each new project in an individual and appropriate way. His work was reactionary to the international style rational formal modernism, i.e. "square box buildings." He was controversial and enigmatic, and his writings were scarce. The work spoke for itself. There were neo-Expressionistic, artistic structures with monumental practical and symbolic forms.

Dulles airport had "suspension bridge cables stretched in a catenary curve and concrete piers sloping out to counteract the pull of the cables … like a huge continuous hammock suspended between concrete trees." *It was Saarinen's best work* and the one that he reportedly claimed to be his best, the one that I would emulate in the Tropiline Bajan Design chair.

Finally, his Gateway Arch's 630-foot-high parabolic arch for timeless monumentality and contemporary dynamism had classic Nordic elegance and served as the gateway to the West.

Gateway Arch, St. Louis, Missouri

The Gateway Arch for its brilliant simplicity was a parabola. With the methods of production I had available in the various prototypes, I was only able to get two angled columns and an arch on top, not a true parabola, which is a continuous curve. Also, the fact that one line solved the design problem is another strong influence from Saarinen, who, for this project, would have to be called my "Master."

2. Marcel Breuer

Marcel Breuer's cantilevered steel chair was influential for its form, simplicity, and the ubiquitous nature of its production and sales. It was affordable for students and average-income workers, very pure in concept, and, even though it was designed in 1928, it still remains today a fresh, modern design that has not aged. This quality is one that I desired in my chair design. The idea was brilliant concept, affordable, available, and one that would not be dated in a few years.

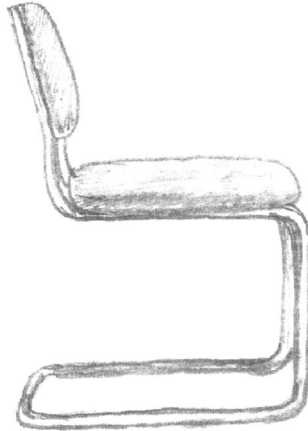

Breuer Chair

3. Le Corbusier

From Le Corbusier's Villa Savoye, Chandigarh, and Carpenter Center we learn massing, modeling, manipulation of light, the plan as generator, the section as structural and circulation system, and the elevation as elevation of the plan/section (mainly). There should be no applied ornament, decoration, carvings, or the like. It was brutal use of sculptural form, brilliant light, and innovative spaces. *Good form was quite enough.* A good-looking building/design is like a good-looking woman: well-structured, and with the minimum amount of applied ornament.

From Corbusier's *Towards an Architecture*, we learn that engineers were attaining harmony, the plan is the generator, and architecture is a plastic thing. Passion can make drama out of inert stone. The plan proceeds from the inside out; the exterior is the result of an interior. Also we see that the plan is the generator of volume and surface and that it irrevocably determines everything. His famous quote is "Architecture is the masterful, correct, and magnificent play of volumes brought together in light." The plan demands the most active imagination. It also demands the most severe discipline. The plan carries with it the very essence of the sensation.

Regulating lines fixes the fundamental geometry of the work. Contour modulation is the touchstone of the architect...it calls for the plastic artist. Emotion comes from the unity of intention, unifying relationships, and a sense of harmony. Passion, generosity, grandeur of soul—so many virtues that are inscribed in the geometries of the contour modulation; quantities manipulated into precise relationships were in discussions about the Parthenon in Greece! I visited the Parthenon on a study tour in 1984 and was able to experience the magnificence of these ruins and saw why Western architects go there as their must-see architectural "mecca."

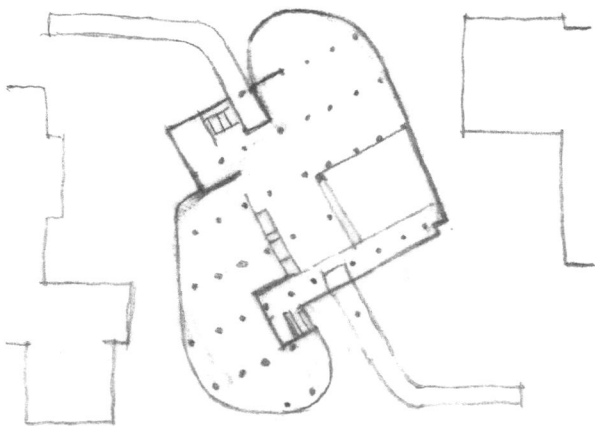

Carpenter Center, Harvard Massachusets

Cruise Ship

4. Kenzo Tange

Kenzo Tange's plan of the Olympic Stadium (Tokyo, 1966) has rotational symmetry in plan and tensile structure in elevation. It was a major influence in terms of form and the need to explore new boundaries of expression. It has cables, sweeping curves, and sculptural concrete form. This is a very dramatic building in section, plan, and elevation. Spatial brilliance is the result with almost organic, reptile-like elements moving freely in space!

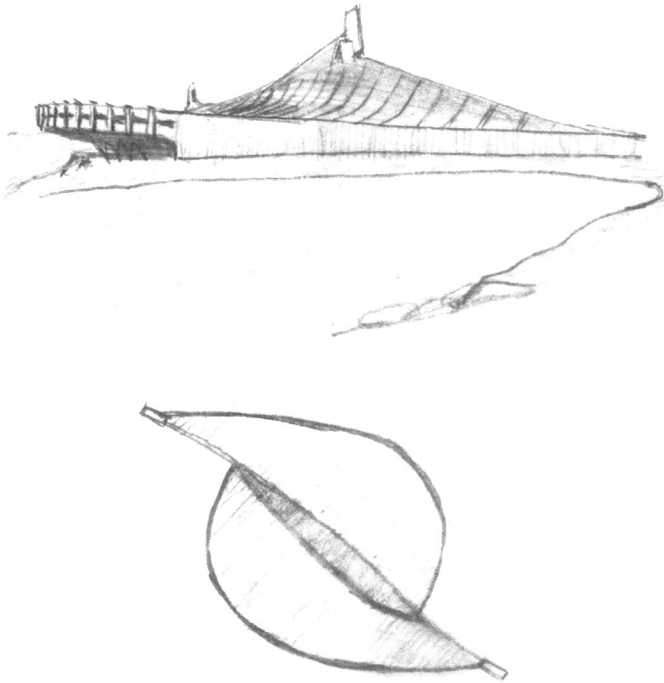

Olympic Stadium, Tokyo

5. Isamu Noguchi

The Noguchi Coffee Table has rotational symmetry in plan. It has clear-form modern design balance and poise. However, this is one of the most complex rotational symmetry designs ever, as explained below. For symmetry, it is really what transformations one has to do to get one side (element) to look exactly like the other. For reflective symmetry, just use a mirror and that is all. Noguchi transformations are as follows:

- There are two identical abstract pieces of panels, cut from one form, with a flat back and two points on the other side.

- The smaller point we will call the chest and the larger point the legs.
- Place one panel vertical with the back to the ground facing east-west.
- Take the other panel and place it next to the first and then turn it upside down.
- Rotate the second panel ninety degrees so that it now faces north-south.
- Connect the first upward-facing chest to the second now down-facing chest.
- Place a see-through rounded triangular glass top on the back of panel two and rest it on the upward-facing legs of panel one.

As you can see, it is a 180-degree vertical rotation followed by a ninety-degree horizontal rotation that gives the final balanced and poised rotational symmetry. *This is brilliant; design does not get any better than this (twin rotational).* We respect Noguchi for his contribution to modernism and sculptural industrial/furniture designs that are as much art as they are furniture. I used rotational symmetry in the Tropiline Bajan Design, where if you do a 180-degree horizontal rotation about the center, one side replicates the other (single rotational).

Noguchi Coffee Table

Mid-Town Manhattan, New York

Guggenheim Museum, New York

Chrysler Building, New York

6. Butterfly (Sling) Chair

The "Sling Chair" by Jorge Ferrari-Hardoy, Juan Kurchan and Antonio Bonet has canvas slung over a metal frame, four apexes, and clumsy form of the metal, especially when folded, and is functional *but not very artistic* without the canvas top. The frame looks visually weak and frail, and it is not considered appealing abstract art without the fabric top.

My roommate had one of these in the dorms at art school in New York, so I saw it all the time. The corner pockets that fit over the frame-like pouches are the method that I used to fit the canvas over the frame. Also, this chair was available in leather as well, which gave a luxury feel and some upward mobility to the design.

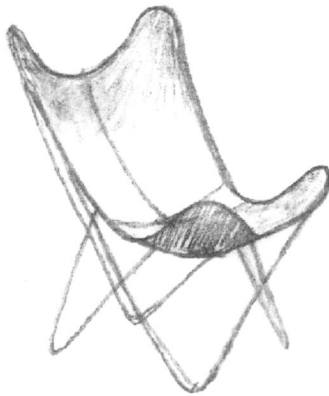

Butterfly (Sling) Chair

7. Pier Luigi Nervi

Pier Luigi Nervi used sculptural form and expressive structure in his Italianate designs. *Architecture as brilliant structure and nothing else!* Engineers and contractors probably have nightmares trying to figure out how to structure and build these buildings. Sometimes architects and engineers had to invent the method of construction when developing a new modern sculptural structural design.

Exhibition Building, Italy

8. Oscar Niemeyer

Oscar Niemeyer was a sculptural form-giver from South America using tropical modernism with drama and allowing terrain to influence the form—*Le Corbusier meets Brazil terrain and culture!* His philosophy in terms of climate, terrain, culture, and geographic location influences on modern structural/spatial form was legendary. He was a master of form, color, and light. The rhythmic, sensuous lines of Brazilian modernism were as legitimately modern as the rectilinear lines of the Bauhaus. He was imagining and responding to the beauty and mystery of the natural world. Form can follow fantasy! Modernist concepts were being transformed to other countries, and he was the Brazilian modernist master. "The power of beauty makes us forget injustice" was one of his comments on dramatic architecture in poor living conditions/poverty. It was Niemeyer's Brasilia capital buildings, with their dome and bowl split by twin towers, that impressed me as an architecture student.

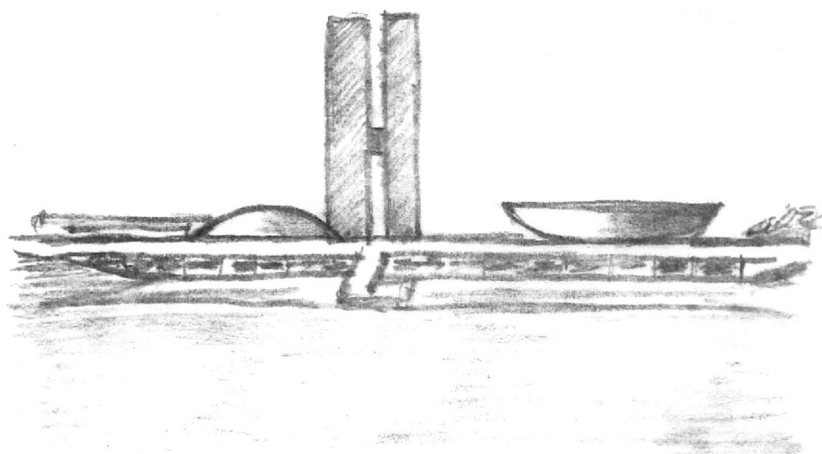

Brasilia, Brazil

Small Gymnasium by Pier Luigi Nervi (top) and Ferrari, Italy

Design Synthesis

The idea for the Tropiline Bajan Design chair was of floating in space with no gravity (NASA-inspired), with the chair as wrap-around anaconda coil, then a zigzag movement under the body to emerge on the other end. Freedom from normal gravitational limitations conceptually, with no vertical columns or normal transfer of weight (load), was suggested. Buildings with angled columns and "plastic"-molded formed concrete in shell-like structures were the influence of the architectural engineering designers or the "form-givers."

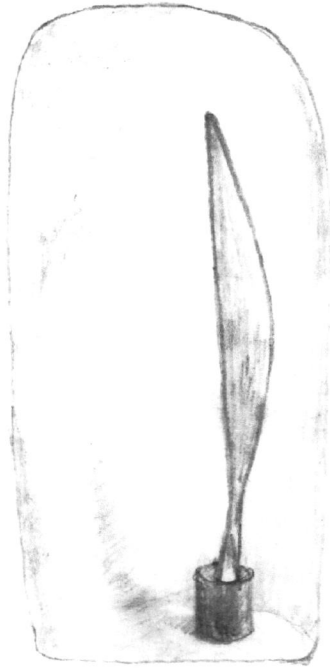

Brancusi's Bird in Space

Tropiline Bajan Design Philosophy

The concept was design as art, not furniture—to be art when the chair not in use and the canvas is removed. A sculptural elemental line in space was used to solve a spatial/structural design problem. There was no attempt to reduce the impact of the sweeping curved seating area by widening the proportions; the dramatic appearance of the slim suspension fabric set on a sculptural tube frame stand was the design. This is lean, efficient and showed a lack of waste in its concept, with an emphasis on frugal use of materials which is modern, progressive, and sustainable, especially for small states design and emerging design markets.

Tropiline at home on Dover Beach, Barbados

Product Development

The tube bending for the frame was done by a local manufacturing company in Barbados around 1990. It was shown to but not licensed by any local manufacturer, as no manufacturer appreciated (or comprehended) the enormous export potential of a product with a USA patent (America having *one thousand times* the population of Barbados). The canvas top was done by various artisans. There was difficulty finding one firm that could produce the entire design, frame and canvas. My experience and successes were in preliminary design, developed design, prototype production, patent preparation, filing, award, and the American component of the latter. Licensing to existing manufacturers was the preferred marketing route. Five years after the USA patent expired and the product became generic, the Chinese began producing a few prototypes. Off-patent, high-volume production happens in the pharmaceutical industry all the time because of the age-defying value of the formulation. *The aim was to do this for the furniture / hammock frame.*

Chevrolet Camaro

Colors and Finishes

The original prototype was baked in a beige factory finish. In fact, I was at the factory when it first came out and remember seeing it coming out of the paint oven and saying it was like the birth of a child. I repainted it red and then white by hand at different times to get different pictures for promotion. I remember getting roofing compound—a thick plastic paint—to provide a rust-proof finish for the steel, as I was concerned that it would rust in outdoor situations. The original canvas was green military-style tent canvas. Then I got some yellow-and-white-striped canvas for a more nautical beach outdoor appearance, but the material was lighter in weight/strength. This was fabricated by another local tailor/seamstress.

Tropiline Prototypes at home in Barbados

USA Patent 1992

United States Patent [19]

Blackman

[11] **Patent Number:** **Des. 328,198**

[45] **Date of Patent:** **..** **Jul. 28, 1992**

[54] **LOUNGE CHAIR FRAME**

[76] Inventor: **Don James B. Blackman**

[**] Term: **14 Years**

[21] Appl. No.: **250,339**

[22] Filed: **Sep. 28, 1988**

[30] **Foreign Application Priority Data**

Mar. 28, 1988 [BB] Barbados 2

[52] **U.S. Cl.** **D6/361; D6/386;**
D6/499

[58] **Field of Search** D6/334, 361, 362, 363,
D6/367, 368, 369, 374, 375, 500, 386, 387;
5/120, 127, 128, 130

[56] **References Cited**

U.S. PATENT DOCUMENTS

D. 169,338	4/1953	Risley	D6/369
D. 171,176	12/1953	Yellen	D6/375
D. 172,068	4/1954	van Derbeken	D6/374
D. 177,783	5/1956	Witty	D6/367
D. 190,909	7/1961	Banyard	D6/361
D. 261,332	10/1981	Rohr	D6/363

Primary Examiner—Donald P. Walsh
Assistant Examiner—Gary D. Watson
Attorney, Agent, or Firm—Kenyon & Kenyon

[57] **CLAIM**

The ornamental design for a lounge chair frame, as shown and described.

DESCRIPTION

FIG. 1 is a perspective view of a lounge chair frame showing my new design;

FIG. 2 is an end elevational view, the opposite end being a mirror image thereof;

FIG. 3 is a side elevational view, the opposite side being a mirror image thereof;

FIG. 4 is a top plan view; and,

FIG. 5 is a perspective view thereof.

The dot-dash lines shown in FIG. 1 are for illustrative purposes only and form no part of the claimed design.

Tropiline Patent 3D drawing

Marketing Initiatives

There were marketing efforts to manufacturers over the fourteen years of design patent. There was little success, except in 1997 when the Danish firm SUB-CON made a cobalt blue prototype and tried to produce but had difficulties getting it ready for production.

"Regarding the text about SUB-CON I can add that we had a Danish specialized in tube bending to do a couple of prototypes but the reason that it did not go into production was probably the price and the size of the carton needed sending the product to customers. The prototype was checked in Denmark by Habitat and they were OK with the look and the stability but I think the above reasons made them dump the product." SUB-CON A/S Henrik Heide May 15, 2012

Numerous American and Canadian firms did not agree to produce and market the design from the marketing proposals of Errol Dimock of Lomar Associates (a Canadian international licensing consultant firm). This was for licensing the design for sale in the US with the US design patent newly in place in 1994 (twelve years still to go before expiration):

TEL. (506) 857-1377
FAX (506) 882-4623

879 MAIN STREET
P.O. BOX 1261
MONCTON, N.B. E1C 8P9

L.D. DIMOCK & SON LTD.

June 20, 1994

Tropi Design
P.O. Box 1084
Bridgetown
Barbados, West Indies

ATTENTION: Don Blackman

SUBJECT: Tropi Chair

Dear Don;

Enclosed please find for your information the recent list of manufacturers in the U.S.

and Canada that we have submitted your offers of your product to. We will keep you

informed of any interest shown from any of these companies.

Yours truly,

Errol Dimock

Marketing (licensing) letter

1384 Tyandaga Park Drive
Burlington, Ontario,
Canada, L7P 1N3
Tel: (905) 336-0002 Fax: (905) 336-2250

P.O. Box 1261
Moncton, New Brunswick
Canada, E1C 8P9
Tel: (506) 857-1377 Fax: (506) 852-4623

OFFER

Reference: _____ 658 _____   Date: _____ January 1994 _____

A license to manufacture, market a NEW, UNIQUE HAMMOCK STYLE LOUNGE
CHAIR is available from Licensor in Barbados.

The framework design of this product is a one piece structure, making the
"TROPICHAIR" affordable, appealing, individuals, hotels, resorts, providing sales
appeal and opportunities over a broad market range.

Patents have been issued for the "TROPICHAIR" in the United States.

Available for license world wide.

Prototypes have been made, used, thoroughly tested, full information, drawings and
information available.

- ASSOCIATES -
CANADA: Ottawa, Toronto, Englehart, Ontario; Moncton, New Brunswick; Argentina; Australia; Belgium;
Czechoslovakia; Denmark; Dominica; England; France; Finland; Germany; Ireland; Israel; India; Italy; Japan;
Liechtenstein; Luxembourg; Malaysia; Mexico; Norway; South Africa; Spain; Sweden; Switzerland; Taiwan; U.S.A.

Marketing (licensing) proposal

Halcyon Inc.
6142-T 15th Street East
Bradenton, Florida
U.S.A. 34208

Florida Sunshade Co.
3501 N. Dixie Highway
Fort Lauderdale, Florida
U.S.A. 33334

Sunline Industries Inc.
9970D N.W. 89th Ave.
Medley, Florida
U.S.A. 33178

Hoover Industries Inc.
7260-T NW 68th Street
Miami, Florida
U.S.A. 33166

Brown Jordan Company
Stylume Division
14475-T N.W. 26th Ave.
Opa Locka, Florida
U.S.A. 33054

Kreissle Forge Inc.
7947-T N.Tamiami Trail
Sarasota, Florida
U.S.A. 34243

Fabrionics Inc.
Route 130, South
Camargo, Illinois
U.S.A. 61919

Lafayette Wire Prod. Inc.
P.O. Box 4552
Lafayette, Indiana
U.S.A. 47903

Kay Industries Inc.
2000 Waverly Road
Janesville, Iowa
U.S.A. 50647

Dant Corporation
1500-T Bernheim Lane
Louisville, Kentucky
U.S.A. 40210

Habitant Corporation
809-T East Midland St.
Bay City, Michigan
U.S.A. 48706

Blue Water Ornamental Iron
4430-T Rabidue Road
Goodells, Michigan
U.S.A. 48027

Tandem Products, Rhino-
Hyde Division
520 Industrial Drive
Blooming Prairie, Minnesota
U.S.A. 55917

Structural Foam Plastics Inc.
P.O. Box 5208-T
North Branch, New Jersey
U.S.A. 08876

Telescope Casual
Furniture Inc.
Church Street
Granville, New York
U.S.A. 12832

Bielecky Brothers Inc.
306 East 61st Street
New York, N.Y.
U.S.A. 10021

Cardinal American Corp.
Cardinal Home Products
Division
5185-T Richmond Road
Cleveland, Ohio
U.S.A. 44146

Clinton Metal Products Co.
1076-T W. Locust Street
Wilmington, Ohio
U.S.A. 45177

Calder Manufacturing Co.
1322-T Loop Road
Lancaster, Pennsylvania
U.S.A. 17601

Hill Company
8617 Germantown Avenue
Philadelphia, Pennsylvania
U.S.A. 19118

Tennessee Fabricating Co.
1822-T Latham Street
Memphis, Tennessee
U.S.A. 38106

Elgin Craftsmen Inc.
608-T West Alamo
Elgin, Texas
U.S.A. 78621

Texacraft Inc.
P.O. Box 741558-T
Houston, Texas
U.S.A. 77274

Bromwell Inc.
416-T S. Washington Street
Falls Church, Virginia
U.S.A. 22046

Miller Manufacturing
Company Inc.
Stockton Street, 6th & 7th
Richmond, Virginia
U.S.A. 23224

Twin Oaks Hammocks
Route 4, P.O. Box 169
Louisa, Virginia
U.S.A. 23093

US Firms list

Bemis Manufacturing Co.
300 Mill Street, Dept. L
Sheboygan Falls, Wisconsin
U.S.A. 53085

American Metal
Products Inc.
2905 North 35th Avenue
Birmingham, Alabama
U.S.A. 35207

Birmingham Stove & Range
Company
P.O. Box 2647
Birmingham, Alabama
U.S.A. 35202

American Leisure Designs
P.O. Box 2000
Greenville, Alabama
U.S.A. 36037

J.F. Day & Company Inc.
2820 6th Avenue South
Birmingham, Alabama
U.S.A. 35210

Meadowcraft Inc.
P.O. Box 1357
Birmingham, Alabama
U.S.A. 35201

Flanders Industries Inc.
1901-T Wheeler Avenue
P.O. Box 1788
Fort Smith, Arkansas
U.S.A. 72902

O.W. Lee Company Inc.
930-T North Todd Avenue
Azusa, California
U.S.A. 91702

Shaw Creations Inc.
2124 Adams Avenue
San Leandro, California
U.S.A. 94577

Annapolis Forge & Foundry
P.O. Box 250
Annapolis Royal, N.S.
B0S 1A0

Avenger Designs
P.O. Box 712
Oakville, Ontario
L6J 5C1

Bonar Inc.
311 Alexander Avenue
Winnipeg, Manitoba
R3A 0M9

Casual Industries Inc.
P.O. Box 616
Grand Bend, Ontario
N0M 1T0

Designer's Alley Corp.
P.O. Box 455
Orillia, Ontario
L3V 6K2

Ethier Welding Ltd.
P.O. Box 767
Falher, Alberta
T0H 1M0

Fibre 3K Ltd.
55 Daoust, #102
St-Eustache, Quebec
J7R 6P4

Fibreweave
Manufacturing Ltd.
7909 Argyll Road
Edmonton, Alberta
T6C 4A9

Gracious Living
Industries Inc.
2740 Steeles Avenue West
Concord, Ontario
L4K 4T4

Bob's Bikeworks
Gray's PVC Furniture
Division
357 Bannatyne Avenue
Winnipeg, Manitoba
R3A 0E3

Heidt Products Inc.
P.O. Box 8
Waterloo, Ontario
N2J 3Z6

William Les Granites Inc.
137 - 61eme Rang S.
St-Elie D'Orford, Quebec
J2B 8B3

Lindsay Specialty Products
50 Mary St. West
Lindsay, Ontario
K9V 4S7

Smokey Manufacturing Inc.
975 Martin Grove Road
Etobicoke, Ontario
M9W 4V6

Valley Canvas & Awning Ltd.
1383 Ellis Street
Kelowna, B.C.
V1Y 1Z9

Ven-Rez Products Limited
P.O. Box 399
Shelburne, N.S.
B0T 1W0

R.P. Veranda Jardins Inc.
C.P. 233
Drummondville, Quebec
J2B 6E5

US Firms (con't) and Canadian firms

In mid-2001, I left Barbados (and architecture) for good to go to a two-year graduate business school program in the USA, which I completed.

Some three years after I graduated, the USA design patent expired. I was then working in corporate finance in South Florida, USA.

Corporate jet

Copyright of Design, July 2011

A July 2011 copyright application to the US Patent and Trademark Office to use the issued patent for miniatures, souvenirs, or sculptures of any size was denied in October 2011, citing the need for separation between function and aesthetic. The idea was to copyright the line as art and the frame as sculpture and be able to produce miniatures, souvenirs, or large-scale sculptures that would be protected by the copyright that is the same design as the issued patent but with no implied function. Starting the project again, as a generic (off-patent), successful international design product would hopefully generate interest in the design philosophy, where there could be value in its discovery for emerging design communities.

Maserati

Promotion of Design to Manufacturers, July 2011

In July 2011 there was a new drive to get the product on the market as a fresh design off-patent and generic as is common in the pharmaceutical industry.

The idea was that if the chair is off-patent and produced in a generic fashion it could generate buzz and international interest that could translate into interest in the design. Work began on the formal theory and philosophy to fill any demand for information about the design, which is still unique and fresh.

Twenty proposals were sent off to China on July 18, 2011, for producing the chair in China. They had Regular DWGs, Stacking and Stabilizing Spurs (SSS), Open Toe Top, Reinforcement, Three-Piece Version, and Scale DWG for production. The companies included ten hammock frame/casual furniture manufacturers, while another dozen were sent to product design firms, industrial design firms, engineering schools, and business schools in China, plus one Chinese design firm set up in Vietnam. Chinese prototype development was expected for late 2011.

The July 17, 2011 Chinese Proposal

Attn:	Personnel Name Here
	➢ Company name Here

CHINESE/BARBADOS (BAJAN) DESIGN PROPOSAL

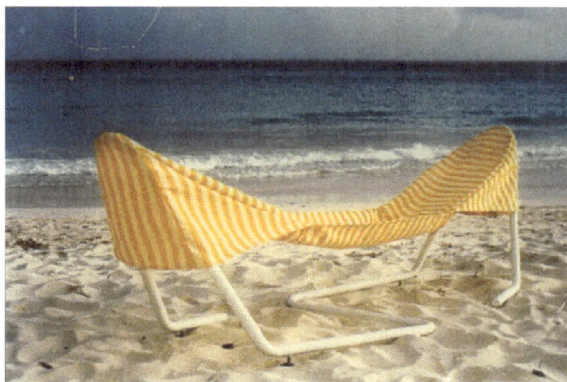

Design Proposal China

July 2011

PART I

From: Don J.B. Blackman
Florida, USA
Contact: donjbblackman
Date: July 17, 2011
Topic: New Bajan Design (off-patent) available for China manufacturing and sale worldwide.

A photograph and a copy of the patent for the chair are shown below. Scaled drawings are also attached. It is a new "luxury/sport" and outdoor furniture/sculpture. The product is a very creative abstract pure line in space, and a fabric cover or "sling hammock" covers the seating area. It is heavily influenced by the modern masters (Gateway Arch and Dulles airport in the USA) and Caribbean exotica. This is a stunning product, the best design ever to come out of the Caribbean. The USA patent expired in 2006, but the design is still new and fresh.

It has been developed in Barbados, Antigua, New York, and Miami. I assure you there is no other like it in the world. Patios and balconies in Rio, Beijing, and Los Angeles would be graced with this.

This early prototype made in Barbados is shown photographed on a beach there. It is the first Bajan industrial design ever to get a USA design patent. My only interest now is to see the product through to successful and profitable quality production for a global market.

United States Patent [19]

Blackman

[11] Patent Number: Des. 328,198

[45] Date of Patent: ᵃᵃ Jul. 28, 1992

US00D328198S

[54] LOUNGE CHAIR FRAME

[76] Inventor: Don James B. Blackman

[**] Term: 14 Years

[21] Appl. No.: 250,339

[22] Filed: Sep. 28, 1988

[30] Foreign Application Priority Data

Mar. 28, 1988 [BB] Barbados 2

[52] U.S. Cl. D6/361; D6/386; D6/499

[58] Field of Search D6/334, 361, 362, 363, D6/367, 368, 369, 374, 375, 500, 386, 387; 5/120, 127, 128, 130

[56] References Cited

U.S. PATENT DOCUMENTS

D. 169,338	4/1953	Risley	D6/369
D. 171,176	12/1953	Yellen	D6/375
D. 172,068	4/1954	van Derbeken	D6/374
D. 177,783	5/1956	Witty	D6/367
D. 190,909	7/1961	Banyard	D6/361
D. 261,332	10/1981	Rohr	D6/363

Primary Examiner—Donald P. Walsh
Assistant Examiner—Gary D. Watson
Attorney, Agent, or Firm—Kenyon & Kenyon

[57] **CLAIM**

The ornamental design for a lounge chair frame, as shown and described.

DESCRIPTION

FIG. 1 is a perspective view of a lounge chair frame showing my new design;
FIG. 2 is an end elevational view, the opposite end being a mirror image thereof;
FIG. 3 is a side elevational view, the opposite side being a mirror image thereof;
FIG. 4 is a top plan view; and,
FIG. 5 is a perspective view thereof.
The dot-dash lines shown in FIG. 1 are for illustrative purposes only and form no part of the claimed design.

PART 2

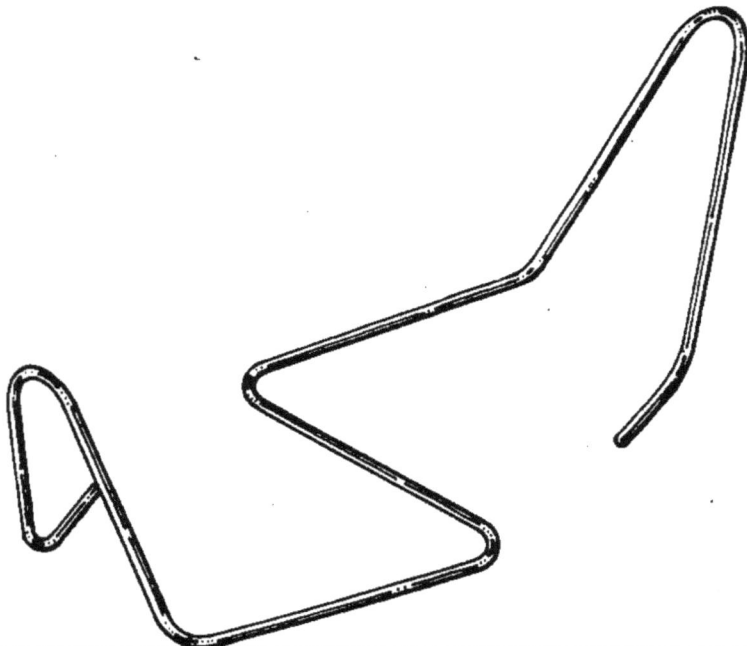

Preproduction Details (July 17, 2011)

(A) Introduction

The attached illustrations show detail on how certain issues relating to the chair can be solved. They are practical, affordable, and easily engineered solutions for Chinese technology. They represent my thoughts on the issues but are not exclusive. In fact, I welcome suggestions from you.

(B) Reinforcement

Because of the "S"-shaped plan of the design, a considerable amount of the load of an occupant ends up twisting the center of the tube in the "S" crossover section. To reinforce this there are a number of methods. Figure 1 shows the use of a solid steel bar or "backbone" that is slid into the open twenty-foot tube, welded to the outer tube through a small hole, and then bended with the outer tube to form the shape of Figure 2. This method allows the reinforcement to be invisible to the user, while giving the assurance that the design's center will be solid and durable, allowing structural failure at extreme loads to shift to the arches and the canvas, which would fold in and lower to the ground, respectively. I like this low-cost option for the one-piece (external) single line chair.

(C) Stacking & Stabilizing Spurs "SSS"

The stacking and stabilizing spurs in Figure 3 allow the chair to stack for cases where the users have more than one and would like to conserve storage space. This is also good for hotels, cruise ships, and commercial properties where the users may want to stack the chairs in a corner for guests for special functions. The stabilization aspect is for the regular seven-foot design, not so much for the user (since their center of gravity falls inside the base and therefore forms a static structure in equilibrium) but mainly to prevent tipping if another person rests on the chair from outside when it is empty. This is a low-cost but effective safety device.

(D) Three-Piece Design

The three-piece design in Figure 4 solves the problem of reinforcing the center in a very clever way and is a favorite since it also allows for easier manufacturing, much smaller packaging for shipping, easier storage in smaller spaces, and can be taken home in a 3'x 4'x 1'-6" box by users in their car. It uses a larger diameter 1 ¾-inch diameter tube for the center giving the additional reinforcement required then slides two identical arches in the ends of the tubes to complete the design. A bolt fixes each end in place. This has all the style of the design with added practicality. The manufacturer benefits by having more easily formed sections, since the center is now a two-bend tube, and the two ends can be set up to be produced in a way that quality control would ensure identical three-bend tubes for uniformity. It is probably easier to consistently produce perfect examples of the design in three sections every time than producing the overall one-piece complex shape with eight bends in one tube. I believe this is a very practical and inexpensive version to produce.

(E) Fabric Tops

The standard top in Figure 5 is made of heavy-duty canvas put on the frame by use of a zipper and three buckles at one end. The buckles are an extra safety measure to prevent the top from sliding off if the zipper fails. There is also an open-toe version in Figure 6 (I am sorry for the reference to ladies' shoes) that allows users to put their feet down straight instead of up as with the standard hammock. The open-toe version allows for the positioning of a "Gateway Arch" handle, a one-inch diameter tube that sweeps over the chair, as shown in Figure

6, allowing the user to hold onto it for ingress and egress. This is a response to customers saying that they had difficulty getting in and out of the chair. Another fabric option would be to produce the design in leather over the canvas top, where the leather is nonstructural but used to get a softer and more luxurious finish. This would appeal to decorators and discerning customers who want the extra distinction that the luxury of leather brings.

(F) Exotic Metals

A customer who wants the leather top may also want a more elaborate finish to the metal. **Stainless steel** is a good choice for marine exposures, yachts, and distinctive properties. It can be finished in a matt brush textured finish. Limited edition **Brass** and **Bronze** (**Gun metal**) designs can also be made for a higher price. These can be larger at about ten feet long from a one-piece thirty-foot tube with the internal reinforcement bar. This customer would get autographed tops, certificates of authenticity, inscribed and dated frames with the designer's or firm's name, optional finishes, and a spectacular presentation, perhaps sold in different stores from the regular design. I am doing the Toyota Camry/Lexus ES 300 thing here—same chassis but different materials, finishes, design changes, colors, promotions, and price, leading to enough product differentiation to entice a different customer (at a different price). This can be successfully implemented as phase two of the project or the "Lexus" phase after the initial "Toyota" phase.

(G) Conclusion

The purpose of the previous paragraphs is to highlight the issues that a **serious manufacturer** would have when considering producing the chair for profitable sale to the public. I have given options and scenarios that range from the lowest cost, to the most practical, right up to the most exotic and exclusive. Again, these are not meant to be cast in stone but serve to show the range of this great product, which has not been produced; I am hoping that the capitalist in the reader will spur some action and dialogue.

This is a different style of working—South/South cooperation (China/Barbados)—like when I was an architect for a project with contractors **China State Cooperation** from 1999 to 2000 at Ellerslie School in Barbados. I had very good relations with Mr. Wong, Mr. Xie, and other managers and engineers and saw your tenacity, industriousness, and never-give-up attitude firsthand. The Chinese just opened the world's longest bridge at Jiaozhou Bay (Figure 7); I know Chinese are not too timid, shy, or incapable of engineering and producing the world's shortest suspension bridge—my chair—for global *profitable* sale.

Thank you,

Don J.B. Blackman
B. Arch, MBA

Responses from the Chinese Proposal

——Original Message——
From:
To: donjbblackman
Sent: Thu, Aug 4, 2011 10:49 pm
Subject: About CHINESE/BARBADOS DESIGN PROPOSAL (XXXX XXXXXXXXXXXXX withheld for confidentiality)

Dear Mr. Blackman,

Good day!

Thank you for your proposal. We have pay close attention to your letter. By the way, our sales manager is not here these two days, and we will make further discuss on your proposal.

As we are manufactory, we develop our products as well as produce according to the customers.

I learnt that you were architect, and you have kindly given us a really detailed proposal.

We would appreciate if you please kindly make your point more clear. Do you want us to produce this hammock for you, or do you want to us use your patent, or other meanings.

We are waiting for your early reply.

Thank you in advance.

Best Regards.

XXXXX

XXXXXXXXXX Co.,Ltd

——Original Message——
From: donjbblackman
To:
Sent: Fri, Aug 5, 2011 3:05 am
Subject: Re: About CHINESE/BARBADOS DESIGN PROPOSAL (XXXX XXX CO.,LTD)

Dear XXXX,

Thank you for your gracious reply,

I would like your company to produce the hammock for sale and export for a global market. Since it is off-patent I make no financial claim for this type of production. I would be honored if a company of your quality would make the design, ensuring quality production, workmanship, and attention to detail as I see on your website.

If you would like any other information or clarifications, please do not hesitate to contact me.

Best Regards,
Don Blackman
XXXXX
Florida, USA

Ferrari

Chinese Prototype Photos

January 2012

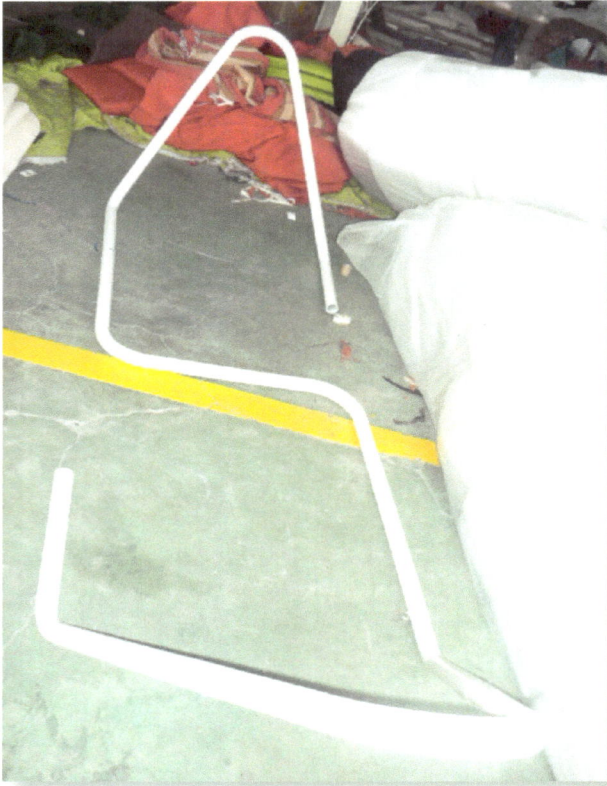

First Chinese Prototype 2012

First Chinese Prototypes 2012

The original Chinese prototype photos were received on January 8, 2012. However, there were some concerns that the design was too low, so they agreed to make another prototype. Photos were received on May 8, 2012, for a second version. This time they also made an oval version that was shown side by side with the Tropiline design.

Second Chinese Prototypes 2012

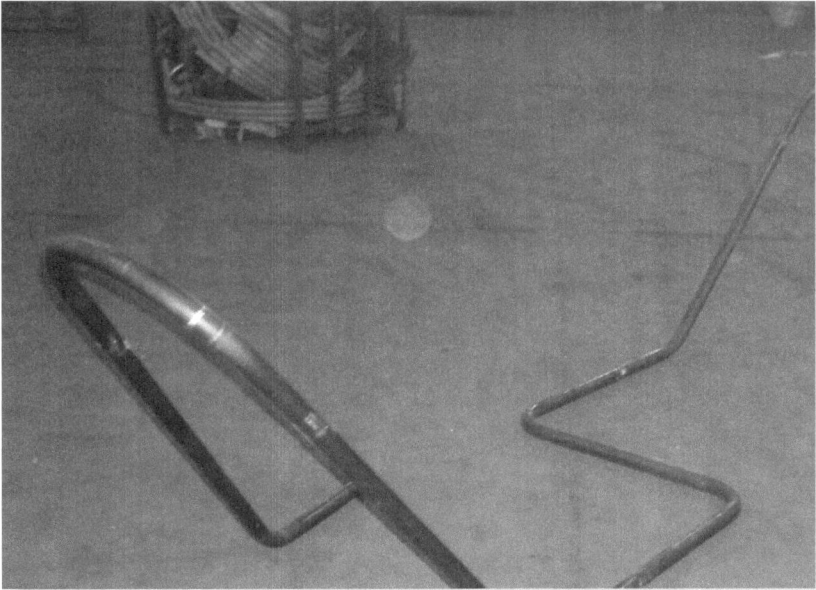

Second Chinese Prototypes 2012

We then agreed that they would try to make the canvas top in white cloth and paint the frame in a natural aluminum/stainless steel color to look like raw steel for a fresh, modern look.

On June 15, 2012, the Chinese sent photos of the new version, which was higher and wider and had a colorful canvas top that looked excellent. But, they had some concerns about the leg part of the design lifting under the weight of the user. I sent an excerpt and a drawing for their consideration that recommended reinforcement for the center and explained the rotation and coiling aspects of the design under load. This was characteristic of the geometry but could be engineered to perform as we desired, as I explained in the "Reinforcement" section (section B) of the original proposal to them sent July 17, 2011.

At the beginning of 2013, the Tropiline remains new and fresh yet still not in commercial production. Artistically, there is no comparable outdoor furniture product anywhere, and very few interior furniture designs could compare.

Second Chinese Prototype 2012 complete with Canvas top!

Closing Argument...Modernism Lives

Modernism lives: emerging markets and Third World cultures need to bring their creative talents to the international stage in formal and rigorous ways using pure, unapologetic, modernist design principles. *"Still Less and Still More."*

BMW

Bibliography

Dachs, Sandra, Patricia de Muga, Laura Hintze, and Arne Jacobsen. *Arne Jacobsen: Objects and Furniture Design*. Barcelona, Ediciones Ploigrafa, 2010. Print.

Fiell, Charlotte. *1000 Chairs.* Cologne: Taschen, 2005. Print.

Hess, Alan, and Alan Weintraub. *Oscar Niemeyer Buildings*. New York: Rizzoli, 2009. Print.

La Pietra, Ugo. *Gio Ponti*. New York: Rizzoli, 2009. Print.

Le Corbusier. *Toward an Architecture*. Los Angeles: Getty Research Institute, 2007. Print.

Le Corbusier. *Towards a New Architecture*. Lexington: BN Publishing, 2008. Print.

Parks, Peggy. *Building World Landmarks —The Sydney Opera House*. Farmington Hills: Blackbirch Press, 2004. Print.

Roman, Antonio. *Eero Saarinen: An Architecture of Multiplicity*. New York: Princeton Architectural Press, 2003. Print.

Venturi, Robert, Vincent Scully, and Arthur Drexler. *Complexity and Contradiction in Architecture*. New York: "The Museum of Modern Art, New York," 2002. Print.

Wilk, Christopher. *Marcel Breuer Furniture and Interiors*. New York: "Museum of Modern Art, New York," 1981. Print.

Zhongjie, Lin. *Kenzo Tange and the Metabolist Movement: Urban Utopias of Modern Japan*. London: Routledge, Taylor and Francis Group, 2010. Print.

Credits

All New York City building photos and car pictures are by Russell R. Blackman. All drawings and illustrations are by the author, except the USA patent drawing, which was produced by/for the noted attorneys.

Don J.B. Blackman is a qualified professional architect and finance manager. He lives in South Florida.

www.ingramcontent.com/pod-product-compliance
Lightning Source LLC
Chambersburg PA
CBHW041214270326
41930CB00001B/16